Science
START HERE!

SUN, RAIN, AND MYSELF

John Stringer, John Paull and Carole Whettall

Sun, Rain, and Myself is based on programmes in the *Science – Start Here!* television series for schools produced by Central Independent Television plc.

Thomas Nelson and Sons Ltd
Nelson House   Mayfield Road   Walton-on-Thames
Surrey   KT12 5PL   UK

51 York Place   Edinburgh   EH1 3JD   UK

Thomas Nelson (Hong Kong) Ltd
Toppan Building 10/F   22A Westlands Road
Quarry Bay   Hong Kong

Thomas Nelson Australia
102 Dodds Street   South Melbourne   Victoria 3205   Australia

Nelson Canada
1120 Birchmount Road   Scarborough   Ontario
M1K 5G4   Canada

© **John Stringer, Carole Whettall, John Paull**

Science – Start Here!
logo and programme material

© 1987, 1988 Central Independent Television plc

First published by Thomas Nelson and Sons Ltd 1988

ISBN 0-17-423104-0
NPN 987654

Printed in Hong Kong

All rights reserved. No paragraph of this publication may be reproduced, copied or transmitted save with written permission or in accordance with the provisions of the Copyright, Design and Patents Act 1988, or under the terms of any licence permitting limited copying issued by the Copyright Licensing Agency, 90 Tottenham Court Road, London W1P 9HE.

Any person who does any unauthorised act in relation to this publication may be liable to criminal prosecution and civil claims for damages.

Acknowledgements

Penny Bickle p11 top left; J. Allan Cash p1, p12 bottom right, p13 top left, p15 top left and right and middle left and right, p17 top left, p23 top left; Central Independent Television p10 upper left; Jeff Foott/Survival Anglia p17 bottom left; Richard and Sally Greenhill p5; Lufthansa-Bildarchiv p8 lower right, p15 bottom left; Oxford Scientific Films p4 left, p8 top right, p13 bottom left, p19 top left; Science Photo Library Front cover bottom left, p27 bottom row; Tony Stone Worldwide p6 lower left; Thames Water p22 top and inset; John Walmsley Front cover top left, p4 right, p11 lower left, p24 top left and right, p29 top left and middle left, p30 top; ZEFA p6 top left and bottom right, p24 lower left, p29 bottom left; Ed Barber p11 lower right, p14 top right, p18 bottom, p19 right, p23 middle right.

Illustrations and diagrams by David Eaton, Richard Crawford Graphic Design, Martin Salisbury and Celia Canning.

Contents
Ideas developed in each section of this book

For parents and teachers — 4

UNDER THE SUN — 6
The sun is the Earth's major source of heat and light.

All life on Earth depends upon the sun.

Some surfaces absorb heat. Others reflect it.

Some colours absorb heat. Others reflect it.

The sun's light can cause coloured surfaces to change.

We can use the sun to tell the time.

RAINY DAYS — 14
Water is all around us. Rain is part of the water cycle.

Weather can be forecast, and rainfall measured.

Some materials repel water, others absorb it.

Liquids behave as if they have a skin on their surface.

Living things need water.

Water is a useful solvent.

I'M SPECIAL — 24
We all have characteristics in common, but we are all special and unique.

We vary in body shape and size.

Some features are inherited. Some are individual and unique.

All living things breathe.

We show differences in interests and skills.

Furniture and clothing designers need to consider people's sizes.

Creatures from other planets would probably be special too!

INDEX — 32

For parents and teachers

What's so important about learning science? Why is it considered to be a vital part of the primary school curriculum?

The HMI Science Committee said:

> Science, with its emphasis on the study of the environment and concern for direct observation and practical investigation, matches what we know of how children learn.
>
> It can assist pupils to bring questioning minds to their experience of things around them. The teaching of science should seek to develop the processes of scientific thinking.

Science is important because:

- we live in a scientific world.

- children should be encouraged to be aware of their environment, to be interested in its richness and to experience the excitement of recognising its possibilities. In doing so, they develop respect for the world and its inhabitants, understanding that their responsible and humane behaviour can make it a better and more interesting place for all.

- we have a custodial responsibility to care for the land, sea and air, and should leave them better after our presence, understanding our dependency on other forms of life.

- children are naturally curious and we, as adults, should encourage this questioning. The questions are as important as the answers, if not more so.

- above all, science is fun and enjoyable – let's encourage children to appreciate and enjoy their world.

The **Science – Start Here!** books aim to present scientific activities that are:

- relevant and interesting to children.
- building on children's everyday experiences.
- encouraging active classroom and home investigations.
- helping to develop children's scientific skills.

What are these scientific skills? They include the ability to:

- observe carefully, sort and classify.
- ask questions of the 'What would happen if . . . ?' sort.
- suggest explanations and make guesses based on observations.
- design investigations and experiments.
- prepare and use apparatus.
- measure accurately, *although children should be encouraged to estimate* before measuring.
- make decisions on the basis of evidence.
- develop concepts and knowledge. There are fundamental concepts in science, and **Science – Start Here!** embodies many of these and introduces a body of knowledge through which to practise skills.
- communicate findings. **Science – Start Here!** introduces activities that will encourage children to communicate their findings through discussion, illustration, displays and the written word.
- apply knowledge to new situations.

The books' subject areas match the broad areas of investigation recognised by the DES in *Science 5–16: A statement of policy* (1985). They are:

- living things and their environment.
- materials and their characteristics.
- energy and materials.
- forces and their effects.

As far as possible, this book uses materials that are available or readily obtainable at school or at home. In addition, some of the following are needed for one – or occasionally more – of the activities:

Two sealed ice-pops, or two plastic bags of ice cubes
A white sheet
A dark curtain
Ropes and stones
A candle
A small box
Shoeboxes
Tin foil
Old magazines or catalogues
Plastic lemonade bottles
Sand
A pea stick or cane
A sheet of polythene, about 50 cm by 50 cm
Seaweed
A block of soft wood
Cooking oil
Paints
Syrup
Plastic beakers
Talcum powder
Washing-up liquid
Ink or food colouring
A stick of celery
Two flat plastic or glass plates
Flower pots
A thermometer
Coarse and fine gravel
Salt
Sugar
Coffee
Fruit juice
A roll of wallpaper
A tape measure
Bathroom scales
Ink for fingerprints
A stopwatch
Drinking straws
A ping-pong ball
A tennis ball
A feather
A balloon

For many of the materials, there are acceptable alternatives; often, children will think of better ones than you do! If their alternative doesn't work, that, too, is a learning experience – but don't let it lead to frustration.

Note: **The activities in this book have been used with safety and success by many children of primary school age. Nevertheless, parents and teachers are advised to give careful consideration to the supervision of practical work, and to follow the explicit safety instructions given in the text.**

None of the activities in 'Under the Sun' involves looking at the sun. Never look at the sun at any time, either with sunglasses, through smoked glass, or with the naked eye.

The sun can blind you – permanently.

UNDER THE SUN

The sun is an enormous ball of blazing gases. Its inside temperature is 20 million degrees Celsius, and its surface is at 6,000 degrees – sixty times hotter than boiling water. The sun is a million times larger than the Earth, and 300 thousand times heavier.

The sun is our major source of energy. It gives us our light and heat. Without it, there would be no life on Earth.

We live millions of kilometres from this tremendous heat. The sun lights and warms our Earth.

Great clouds of burning gas break off from the sun. They are called solar flares.

NEVER LOOK DIRECTLY AT THE SUN. IT CAN DAMAGE YOUR EYES.

Data file

The Earth travels round the sun every 365 ¼ days. We call the time it takes Earth to go round the sun, a year.

Most years are 365 days. But there is still that annoying ¼ day! So every four years, we have an extra day. What is it called?

The Earth's pattern round the sun is a flattened circle – an **ellipse**. You can draw an ellipse with two drawing pins and a loop of string:

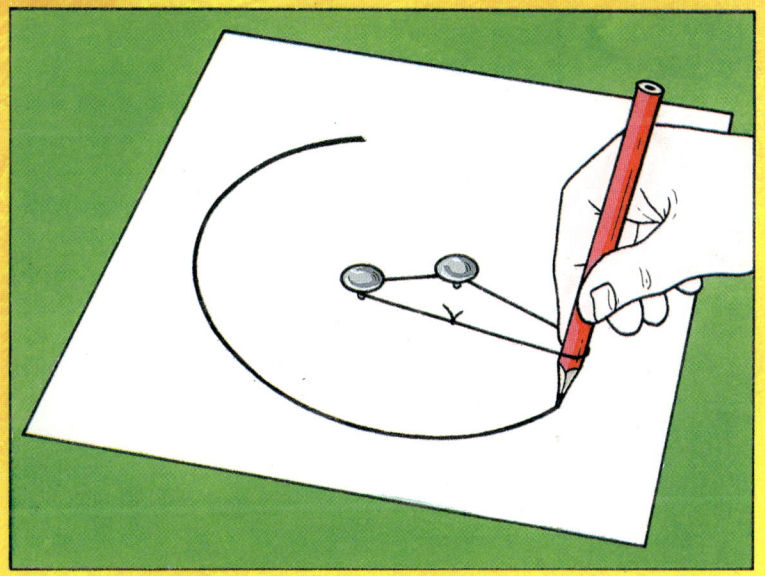

The Earth spins round as it moves along this ellipse. Each spin is a day.

The average distance to the sun is 149 million kilometres. If you could fly there never stopping, at a thousand kilometres an hour, it would take you almost seventeen years.

Our sun is one of 100,000 million stars in the Milky Way galaxy – one of 100,000,000,000,000,000,000,000 stars in the known universe.

And our sun is a very ordinary star . . .

Keeping warm – staying cool

The **solar panels** on this house collect the sun's energy. The sun heats water in the panel, and the water is pumped round the house. It is used for heating and washing.

Why is the panel black?

Take two sealed ice-pops, or two plastic bags with ice cubes inside. Put them in the sun. Cover one with white paper. Cover the other with black – or very dark – paper. What do you notice after half an hour?

Design a suit to keep a polar explorer warm. What colours will you use?

This airliner flies above the clouds. The sun shines on the cabin. Why is the roof white?

Make two tents on a hot day, like this:

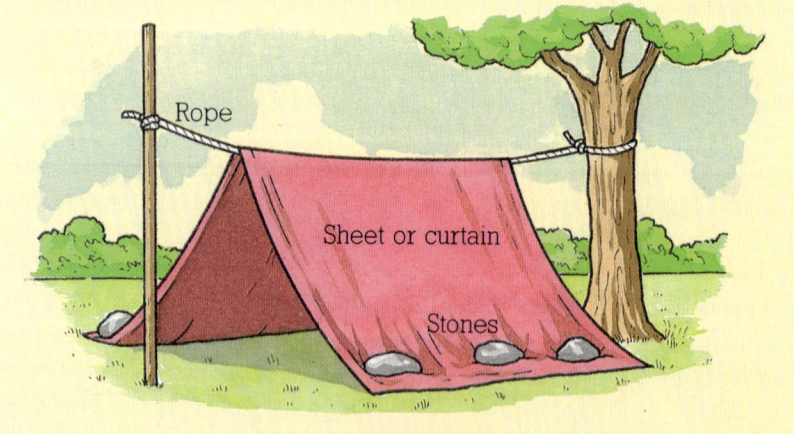

Use a white sheet for one, and a dark curtain for the other.

Go inside both. Which is cooler? Why?

Why are houses in hot countries often white?

Shadows and pictures

We can use the sun's light to make shadows and pictures.

Work with a friend in a big space outside, on a sunny day.

Can you make your shadow:
- small?
- large?
- short?
- long?

Can it have:
- two heads
- four arms?
- three legs?

Can you lose your shadow?

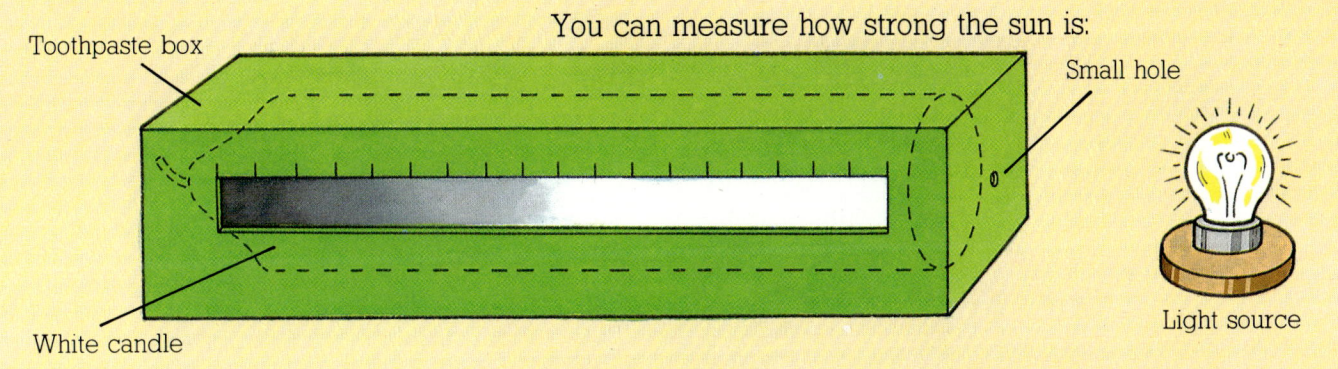

You can measure how strong the sun is:

Toothpaste box
Small hole
White candle
Light source

Point the candle at a bright light. How far does the light penetrate it?

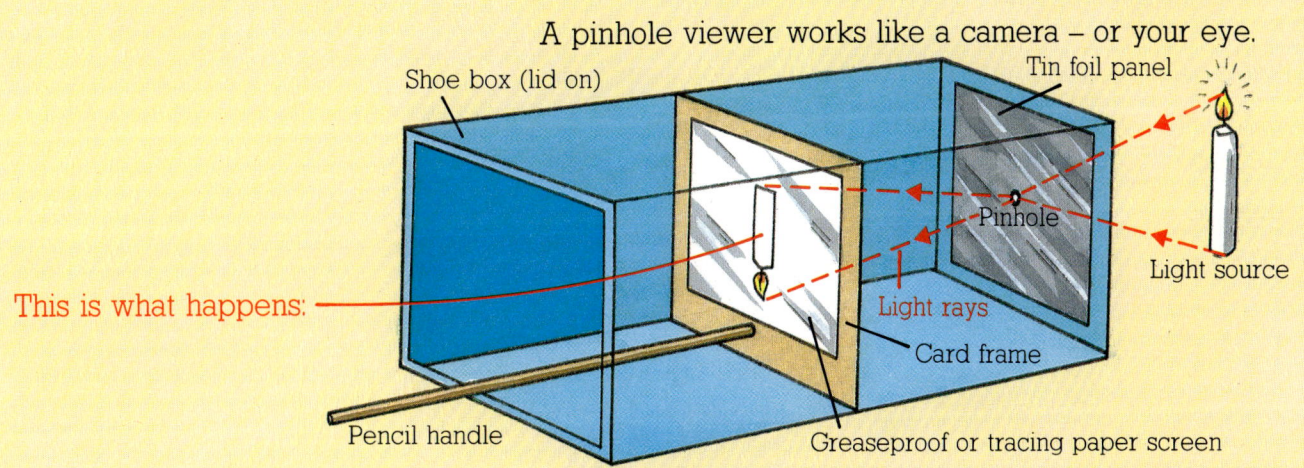

A pinhole viewer works like a camera – or your eye.

Shoe box (lid on)
Tin foil panel
Pinhole
Light source
Light rays
Card frame
This is what happens:
Pencil handle
Greaseproof or tracing paper screen

Point your viewer at a window. Move the screen in and out, slowly. The picture on the screen is called an **image**. What do you notice about it?

Pictures in a camera are taken upside down. Your eye sees things upside down. Your brain learned, when you were a baby, to turn the image the right way up.

DON'T LOOK AT A BRIGHT LIGHT, OR THE SUN.

Seeing a ghost!

Look at something outside the window. Keep looking at it while you count to twenty. Now look away, at the wall.

What do you see? Can you still see the window?

Your eyes grew tired, staring out of the window. When you looked away, the picture took time to fade. But what happened to the colours?

Cut a piece of red paper from a magazine. Put it on some white paper. Look hard at it, while you count to twenty.

Look away, at the white paper. What do you see? Has the shape changed? Has the colour changed?

We call the colour you see the **complementary colour.**

Try different shapes and colours. Try mixing colours – say, a small red piece on a bigger green piece. Record what you see like this:

COLOUR	CHANGED TO	SHAPE	DID IT CHANGE?
RED	GREEN	CIRCLE	X
GREEN		SQUARE	
BLUE			

Fade away

Look around, out of doors, for damage done by the sun. Look at buildings.

Can you find:
- blistered paint?
- faded colours?
- warped wood?

Can you tell which side of the building gets the most sun?

Look inside. Can you find:
- faded curtains?
- faded wallpaper, around pictures?
- peeling paint?
- faded book covers?

Is this the sunny side of the building?

Imagine you arrive at an airport in the desert. Two cars are waiting to meet you. One is black, and one is white. Which car do you choose? Why?
Which is likely to peel more quickly – black paint or white paint? Why?

Do some colours fade faster than others?

Put different coloured papers on a sunny windowsill. Put a small object on each, so they don't blow away. After a week, pick up the objects. Have the colours faded?

Which colour fades fastest?

What's the time?

The Earth is spinning round. Because we are turning, the sun seems to move across the sky. It is low down in the morning, overhead in the middle of the day, and low again in the evening. It disappears at night.

Shadows change through the day.

Put a stick in a plastic lemonade bottle with sand in it. Stand it on a hard surface. Chalk round its shadow.

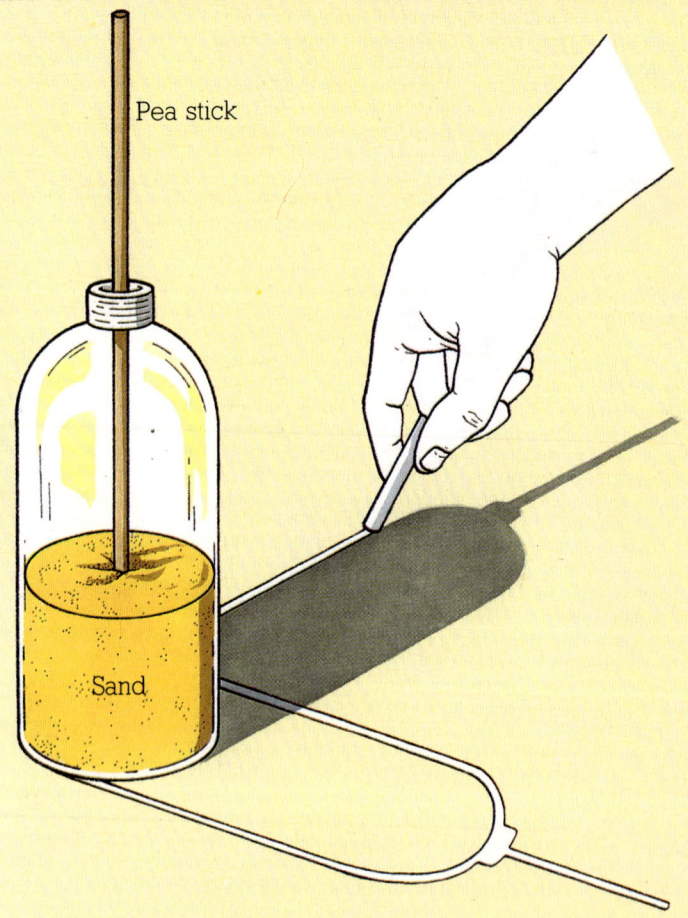

Pea stick

Sand

Come back every hour, and chalk round the new shadow. What do you notice?

A mass clock once told people when it was time to come to church. A pointer throws a shadow across a dial.

Can you make a mass clock? Use a cardboard pointer. Hang it up on a sunny wall.

Does it tell the time?

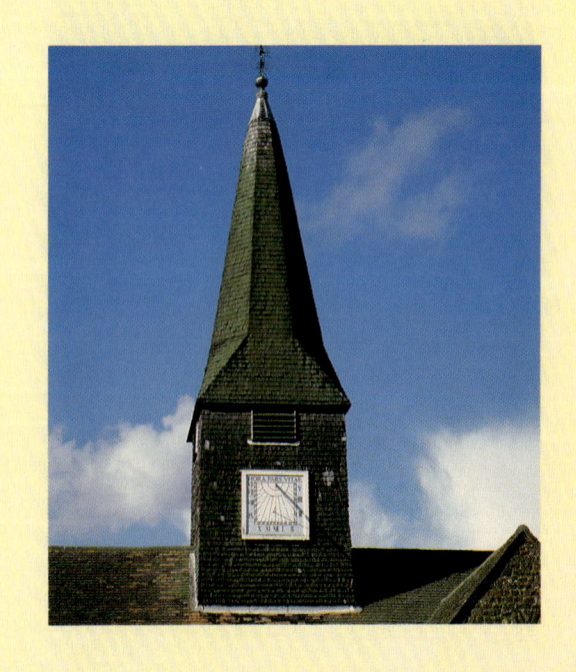

Sundials

The shadow on a sundial points to the time. But sundials need to face in the right direction. So most sundials can't be moved.

An Egyptian sun clock tells the time by the length of its shadow. You can put it down anywhere, facing the sun.

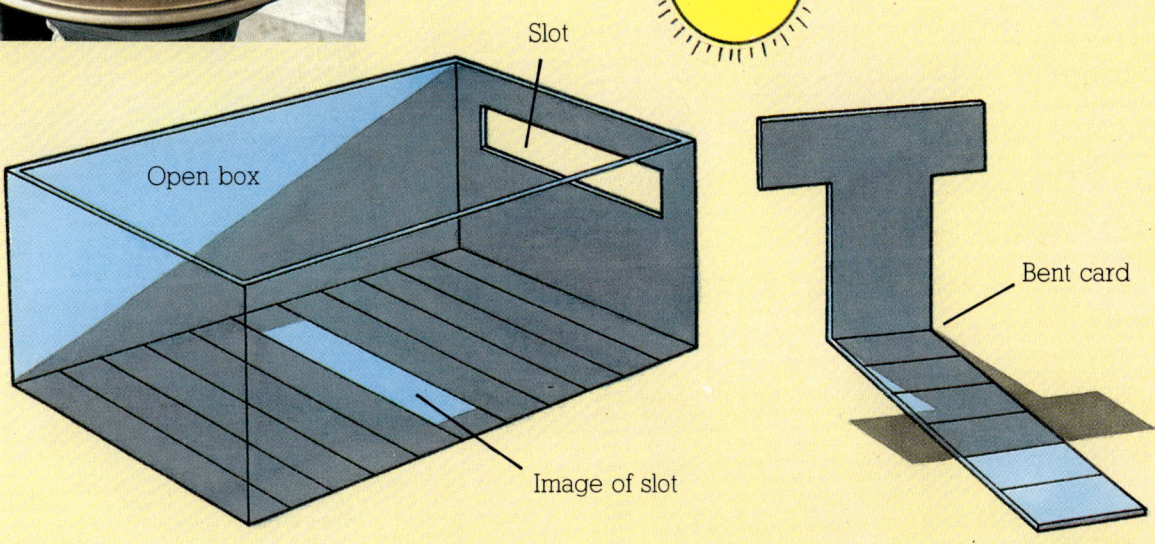

Slot

Open box

Image of slot

Bent card

Set up your sun clock in the morning. Look at your sun clock a little after midday. Why will you have to move it?

Graduate your clock. Draw a scale on it to tell the time.

Look at a sunflower on a sunny morning. Look again later. Has it moved? Where was the sun?

Look at daisies on a sunny day – in the morning, and in the evening. How does the sun affect them?

Can you find how the sun affects other plants?

13

RAINY DAYS

There is water all around. Observe the outside of a *cold* container in a warm room.

This is **condensed** water. It comes from invisible water vapour in the air.

Try using a *warm* container. What do you think makes water vapour condense to water droplets?

How does water vapour get into the air? Try these activities:

Tie a plastic bag around some leaves on a plant. Look again after an hour.

Breathe onto a mirror.

Put out a saucer of water. What happens to the water over a day or two?

The water is **evaporating** into the air. How could you make this happen faster?

Where does the water from wet washing go? Which of these will dry fastest? Why?

Leave polythene spread over the ground on a fine night. What do you notice next morning?

Rain is formed in a similar way. Find out about the **water cycle**.

14

Weather forecasting

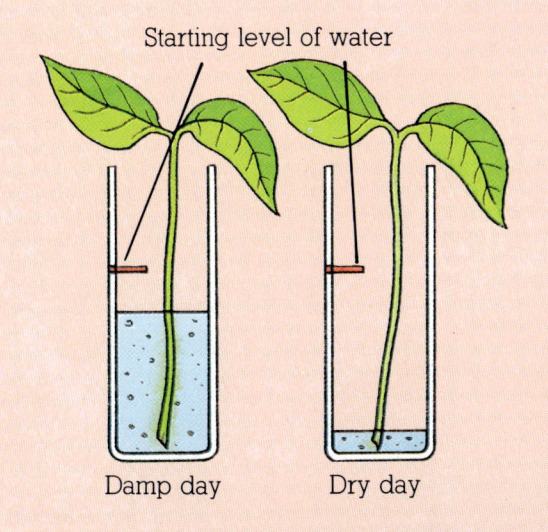

The weather is always changing. Sometimes we can see signs of this happening.

Hang some seaweed outside. It becomes soft in a damp atmosphere, and harder in a dry atmosphere. What happens to a fir cone in moist and in dry conditions?

Plants take up more water in dry conditions.

Clouds form when there is a lot of water vapour in the air. We say the air is humid. Look for these different types of cloud in the sky. What sort of weather follows?

Starting level of water

Damp day   Dry day

Cirrus

Cumulus

Stratus

Nimbus

What do you think the weather is like on the ground beneath this aircraft?

Can you forecast the weather by looking at the clouds?

Sometimes clouds come down close to the ground. Then we have mist or fog.

How much rain?

Try making this rain gauge from a plastic lemonade bottle:

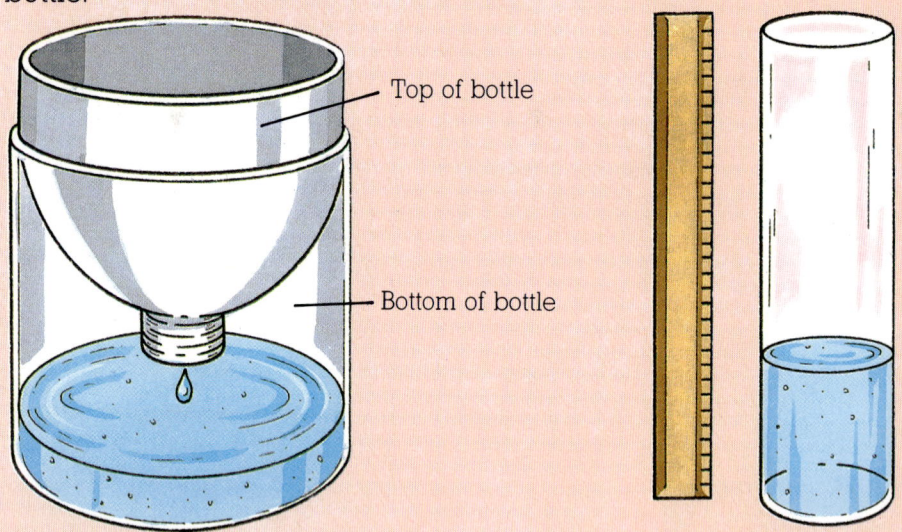

Put the gauge outside in an open place. Make sure it will not fall over.

Measure the rainfall each day. Pour the collected water into a tall, narrow container and measure its height.

Record the daily rainfall on a chart like this:

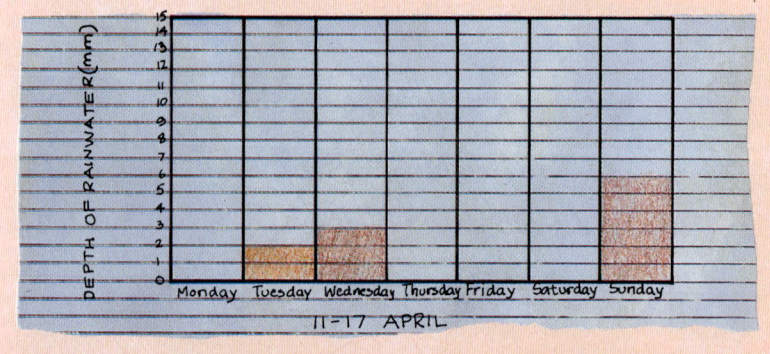

Compare this with rainfall recorded in your local newspaper.

Parts of the Lake District receive over 1500mm (1½ metres) of rain each year. It is one of the wettest places in Britain. Try to find which are the driest places.

More rain falls in mountainous areas. Why?

Clue Air gets cold as it rises and moves over mountain tops.

16

Coping with rain

Rain can make us feel very uncomfortable. Sometimes it brings disaster.

How is rain kept out of your school? Does your school have:

a pitched roof?   damp proofing?
gulleys?   canopies?
guttering?   weather boards?
drains?

Find out how each of these helps to keep the rain out.

In a piece of card, cut a hole *just* big enough to slide over a block of wood (use soft wood). Put the wood in water for 2–3 hours. Will the card slide over it now? What has happened to the wood?

How do ducks keep dry?
How do we keep dry?

What happens to unpainted doors in wet weather? How easy are they to open?

Some things have their own natural protection against water. Can you think of some birds and animals that do?

17

Drips and drops

Drip water from a drinking straw, a pencil or something similar.

What is the biggest drop you can make?
What shape is the drop at the end of your dropper? Does it change as it falls and lands?

Will other liquids make better drops? You could try cooking oil, paint or syrup.

Try dropping water into cooking oil in a clear container. Why does the drop fall more slowly through the oil?

Look at water drops falling onto different surfaces, such as:

- a shiny tile.
- a greasy plate.
- unpolished wood.
- newspaper.
- carpet.

Does the drop break into smaller droplets?
Is it soaked up immediately, after some time, or not at all?
Does the distance the drop falls make any difference to the impact?

This car has been freshly polished. How can you tell?

Surface tension

Drops of liquid act as if they are held in shape by a thin skin, rather like a balloon holding air. This imaginary skin is caused by **surface tension**.

With care you can make a paperclip sit on water.

Carefully fill a plastic beaker with water to just *above* the brim.

Surface tension allows small water creatures, like pond skaters, to walk on water.

Look at the curved water surface. Why doesn't the water spill?

Sprinkle talcum powder onto water in a bowl or a sink. Drop washing-up liquid into the centre. What happens?

Wet your hands. Look at the water on the back of them. Then wash them with soap, and rinse thoroughly. What happens to the water on their backs?

What does soap do to the surface tension of water?

Why do soap and washing powders help water to remove dirt more easily?

Plants and water

How does water keep stems stiff and plants alive?

Stand a celery stalk in coloured water for several hours.
Cut the stalk across into two.
What do you notice?

Water moves up through narrow spaces, like the narrow tubes inside the stem. This is called **capillary action**.

You can see this by standing two plastic plates in coloured water.
Make a narrow gap between them using a matchstick.

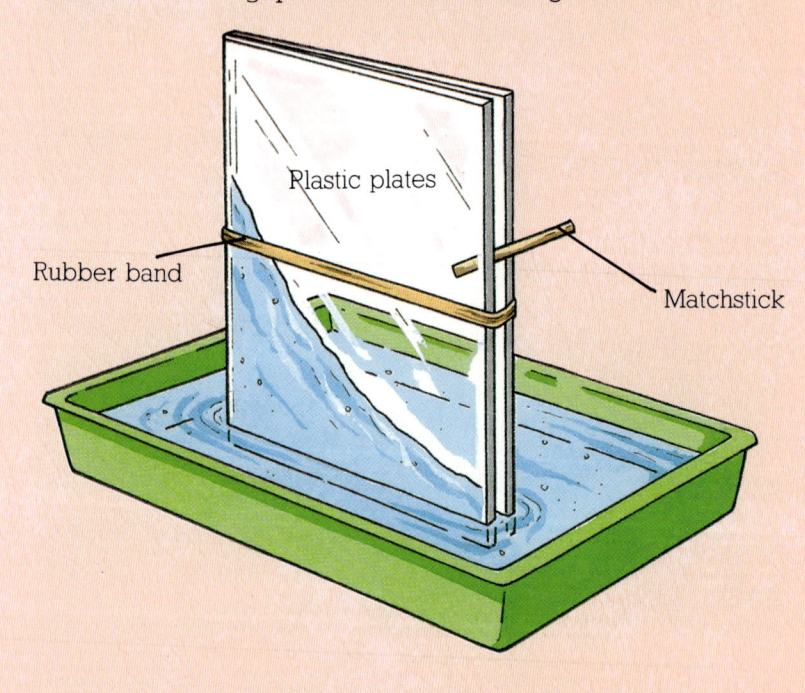

Will a wider gap cause the water to rise higher between the plates?

The spaces between the fibres of blotting paper make it soak up water in this way. Find other materials which behave like this.

This automatic watering device uses the capillary action of water.

Can you design and make another, similar watering device?

Our bodies and water

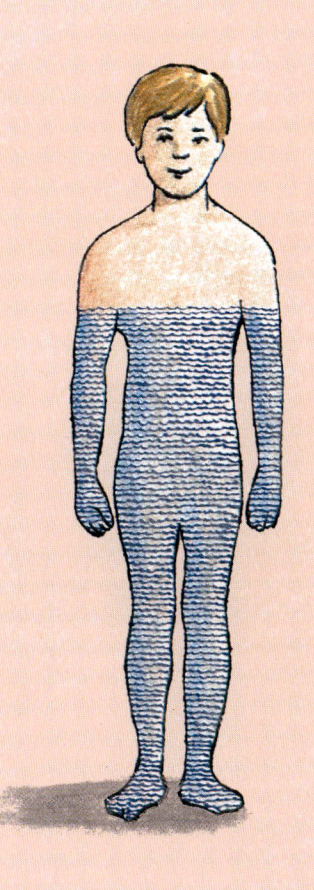

Did you know that two-thirds of your body is water?

Just a few days without water can be fatal.

We lose moisture when we breathe out, sweat or pass waste materials from our bodies. This needs to be replaced daily by 1–2 litres of water.

Use a chart like this to record what you drink each day:

	TEA	COFFEE	MILK	WATER	?	?	?	TOTAL CUPFULS
MONDAY	2 cups	1 cup	—	—				3
TUESDAY	2 cups	3 cups	—	1 cup				6
WEDNESDAY								
THURSDAY								
FRIDAY								
SATURDAY								
SUNDAY								

Which sort of drink do you have most often?
How many litres of liquid do you drink daily, on average? (You will need to find how many cupfuls make one litre.)
Should you be drinking more?

Food contains water too. Lettuce and cucumber are almost entirely water.

Try this:

Wet cover   Dry cover

Which cools fastest?
Why do we sweat when our bodies get too hot?

Pure water

Water from lakes and rivers needs to be purified before we can drink it.

At water treatment works, water stands in reservoirs to allow large bits of debris to sink to the bottom. It is then sprinkled into filter beds like these:

Here smaller particles of rubbish and some **bacteria** (germs) are removed. Finally, chemicals are added to remove any remaining bacteria.

You can make a model water filter like this:

Or try this method of purifying water:

Put muddy water into a bowl. Stand a clean collecting container in the centre.

Drape a sheet of polythene over the bowl and push a hollow in the centre, down towards the container.

Leave for some time in a sunny place.

Clean water will collect in the container. How do you think this happens?

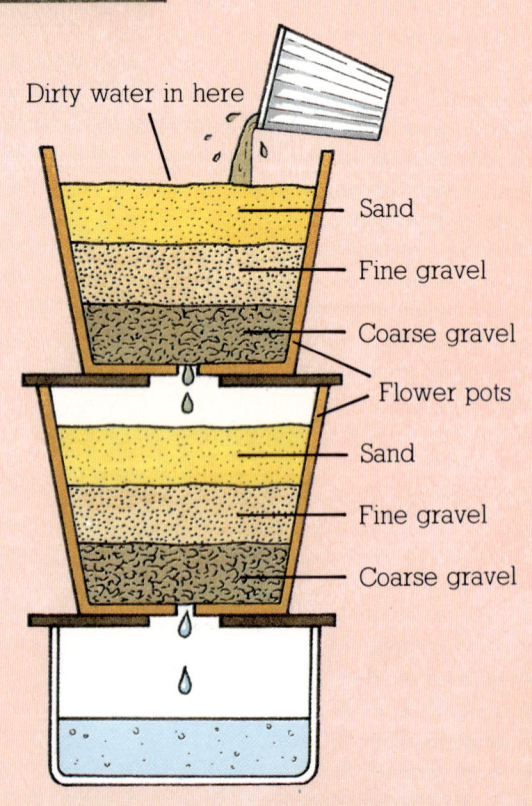

Dirty water in here
- Sand
- Fine gravel
- Coarse gravel
- Flower pots
- Sand
- Fine gravel
- Coarse gravel

DO NOT DRINK THE 'CLEAN' WATER. IT MAY STILL CONTAIN HARMFUL BACTERIA.

Solutions

Stalactites and stalagmites are made by minerals from water that drains through the earth above a cave.

A **solution** is made when a solid dissolves in a liquid. The solid is called the **solute.** The liquid is called the **solvent.**

Water is the most common solvent we know.

Find out which is more soluble, salt or sugar. Does stirring or heating make a difference?

Which substances will not dissolve in water?

How strong is a solution? Make different strengths of coffee with warm water:

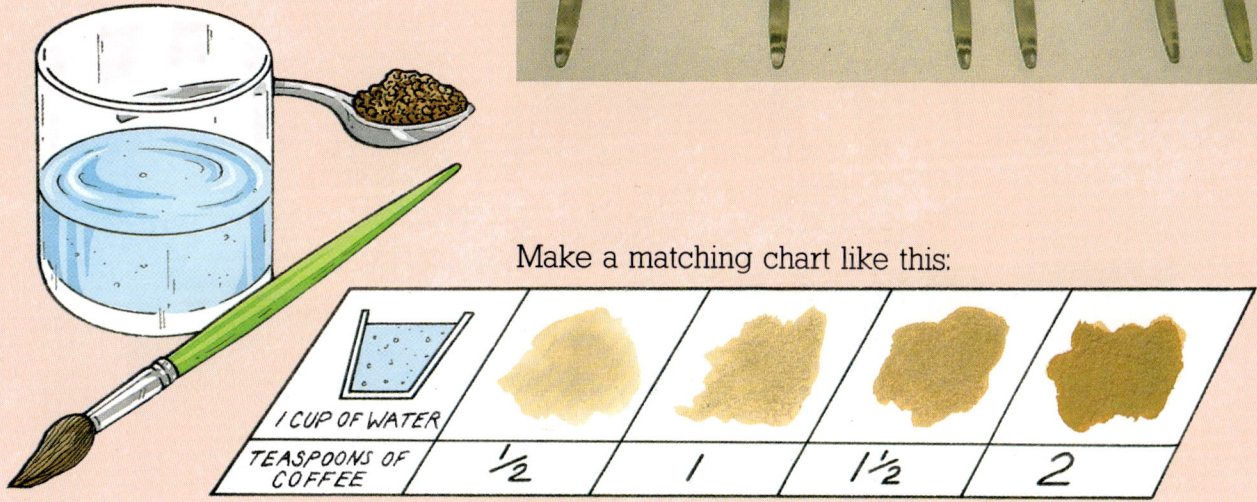

Make a matching chart like this:

1 CUP OF WATER				
TEASPOONS OF COFFEE	½	1	1½	2

Ask a friend to make you a cup of 'black' coffee. Use your chart to find its strength.

Test your friend. You could try diluting fruit juice, ink or food colouring.

Think of ways to find the strength of colourless solutions.

23

I'M SPECIAL

At first sight all the people in a football team look the same.

The numbers on the back of their shirts help spectators sort out the different positions. When the game starts, we can see the differences in the players.

They each have a special job to do during the match.

We are all different, all special, all unique. We have many differences, some that can be measured and some that can't. They make us the people we are.

Look in the mirror. You're special!

Even though there are over 50 million people in Britain, there's nobody just like you.

Height 1.25 m
Chest 66 cm
Waist 58 cm
Arm 56 cm
Leg 55 cm
Weight 26.8 kg

Look at me!

You can make a life-size picture of yourself.
Lie on a big sheet of squared paper and get a friend to draw round you.

Cut out the outline, paste it onto card or wallpaper and colour in the details.

Measure from shoulder to shoulder. How wide are you?

How long are your arms? What colour is your hair?

You can make a data pack about yourself, like this:

"LOOK AT ME" DATA PACK
My name is _____
I am ____ years ____ months old
I live at _____
I weigh _____ and I measure _____
I can stretch _____
My right arm is ____ cm long and my right leg is ____ cm long
My hand measures ____ cm long and is ____ cm across
My right foot is ____ cm long and ____ cm wide
My chest measures _____

My head size is:
WIDTH
LENGTH
CIRCUMFERENCE

Compare your measurements with your friends' and family's.

You could add other special facts to your data pack, such as how fast you can run, or how far you can jump.

What else can you do?

25

Look at my eyes

What colour are your eyes?
How many children in your class have the same colour eyes as you?

Do you wear glasses?

Do any of your friends?
Are they **short-sighted** or **long-sighted**?

You could record your findings on a chart like the one on the right:

Do any members of your family wear glasses?
Are your eyes the same colour as your mother's? They may not be the same as either of your parents' eyes.
Are they the same colour as your grandmother's?

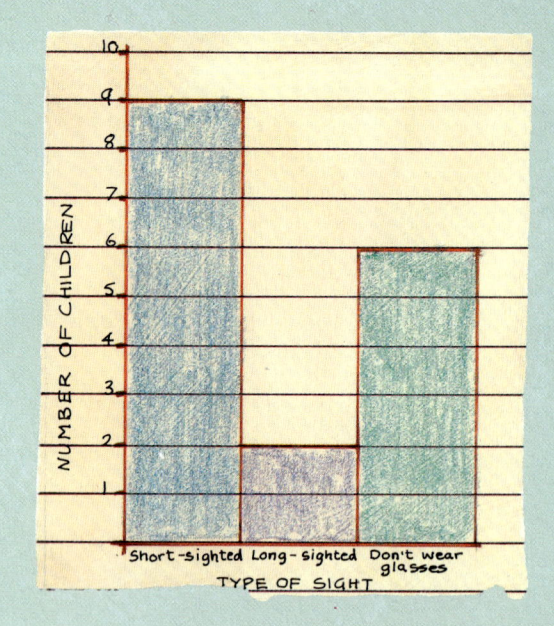

This is my family 'eye' tree:

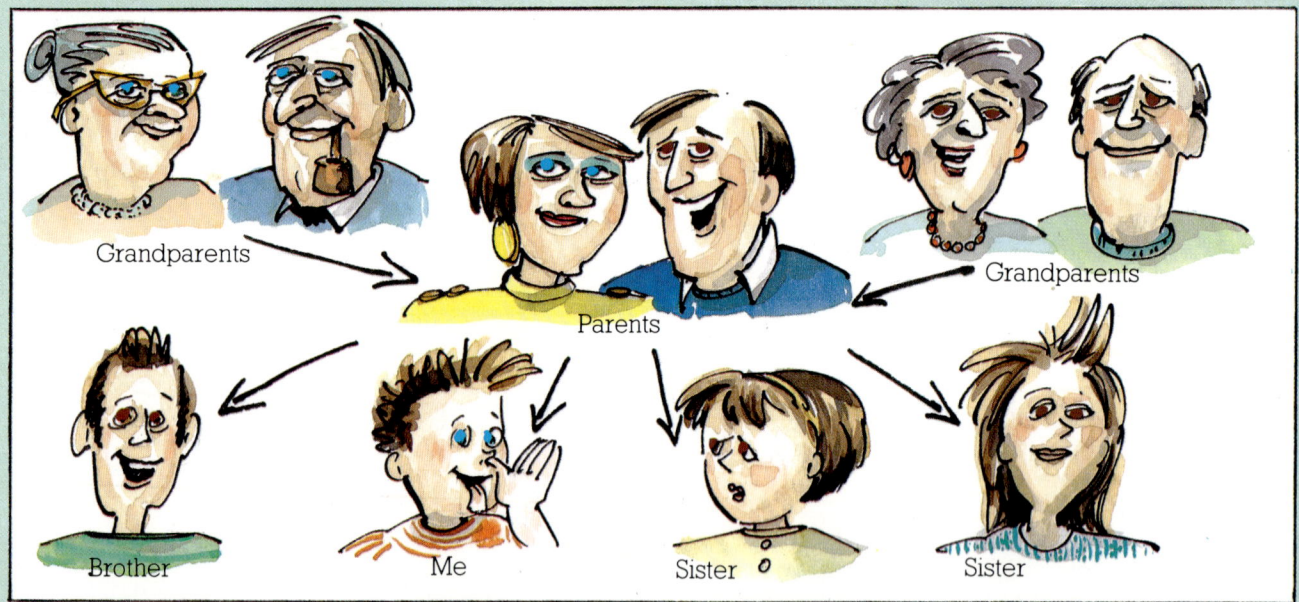

What is your family 'eye' tree like?
Your parents will help you make a family tree.
Perhaps you could use colour photographs.

Where were you born?
Where did your parents come from?
Can you find the places on a map?
Put the information on your family tree.

Can you make a family hair colour tree?

Hands and feet

We use our feet to walk and run, hop and skip, dance and play.

Who has the widest feet in your family?

Can you find three people in your class with the same shoe size?
Do they have the same width measurement?

Take off one of your shoes and put your foot on cm squared paper.
How many squares does your foot cover?
Is the number the same for the other foot?

Try the same activity with your hands.
Is your right hand wider than your right foot?
What do you use your thumb for?
You couldn't walk easily without your big toe. Why?

Can you see your fingerprints?
No two people's are the same. Try making fingerprints and compare them with these pictures:

Arch   Loop   Whorl

Which members of your family have loop prints?

What pattern are your teacher's prints?

Holding your breath

How many breaths do you take in a minute?

One boy estimated that he takes 18,921,600 breaths in a year.
Do you breathe more than that?

Work with some friends and a stopwatch. How many times a minute do your friends breathe before and after exercise? Do their **breathing rates** increase?

When you breathe in deeply, what happens to your ribs?
Does your chest expand? How can you check?

Rest a ping-pong ball on a table.
How far can you blow it? Can you blow it further with a straw?

Can you blow and move a tennis ball?
Can you keep a feather in the air by blowing underneath it?

Using a balloon, can you design an experiment to show how much air you breathe?

Do you know how long you can hold your breath? How do you feel while you're holding it?

Why do we breathe?

Time to relax

Different hobbies interest different people.

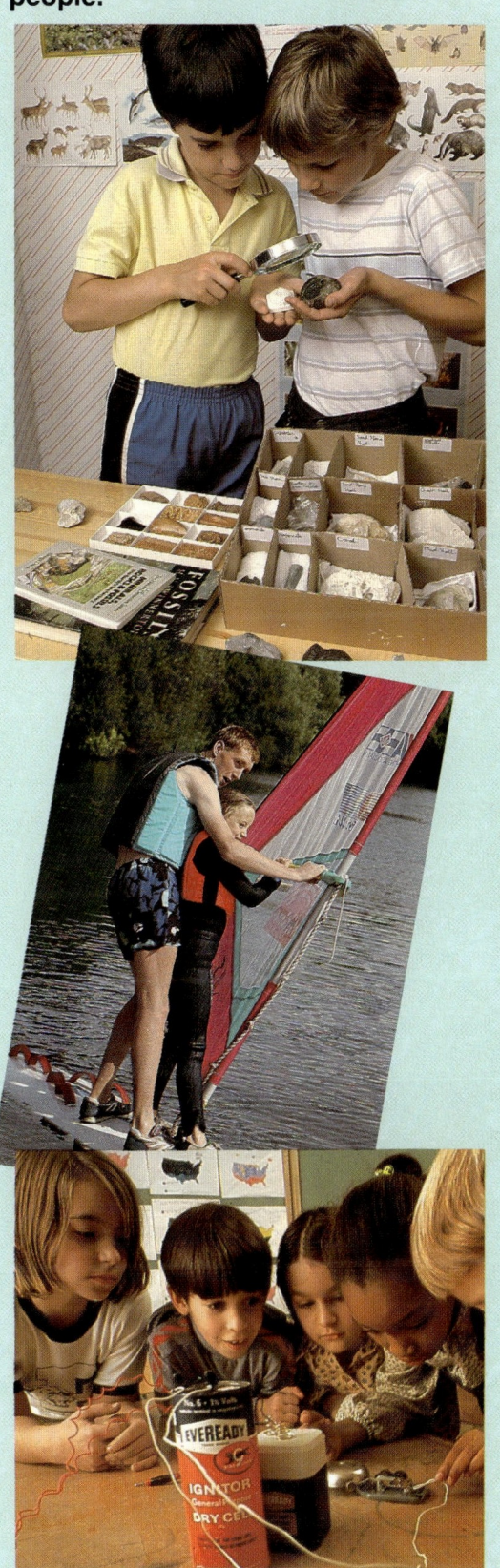

Look at the number of hobby magazines in your newsagents.
The magazines give some idea about people's interests.
Is there a magazine that you buy to help with your hobby?

Are there any science magazines for young people?

What are your hobbies?
Which is your favourite?
Why do you like it so much?
How much time do you spend on it each week?

Hobbies help us learn and relax.
We can learn from each other's hobbies too.
What do your friends do?
How many of them enjoy scientific hobbies?
Make a record like this:

NAME	HOBBY	TIME SPENT EACH WEEK
John	Fossil collecting	Average an hour
Ann	Reading	6 hours
Mary	keeping pets	5 hours

Many athletes started playing sport, and many musicians started listening to music, when they were young. Their skills developed as they became older. Now they play for a living, but still practise hours on end.
Practice makes perfect.

Charles Darwin, a famous naturalist, enjoyed studying small creatures when he was young.
His hobby became his lifetime's work.
Look up his name in an encyclopaedia, and read about his life and his contribution to science.

29

Making it fit

School chairs should be the correct height for you to sit on and work comfortably at a table.

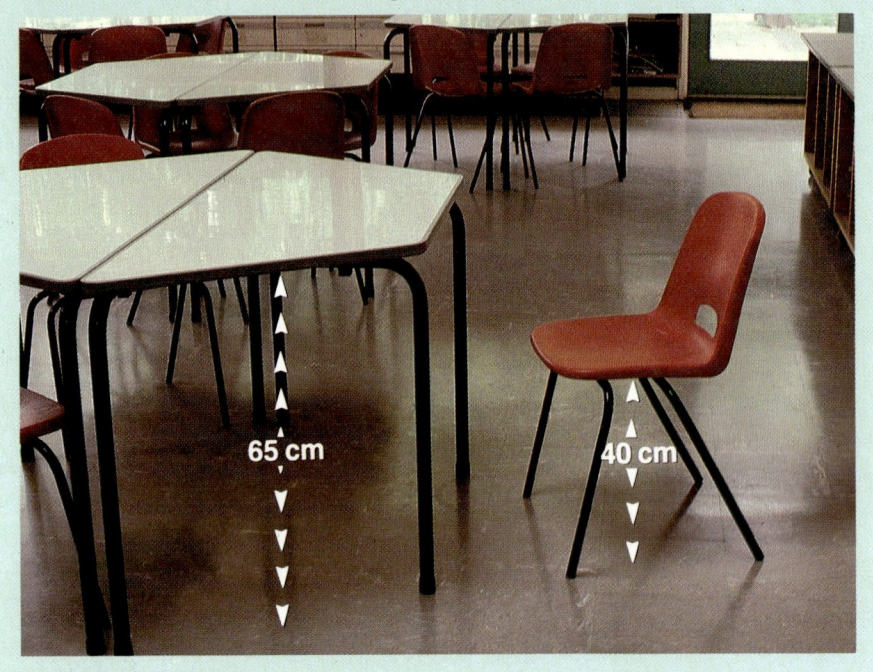

This chair and table have been designed for an 8-year-old pupil.

Is the chair in the photograph the same height as yours?
Do all the children in your class have the same size chair?

Imagine a pupil 3 metres tall!
Design a work table and chair for him or her. First measure yourself and your table and chair.
Why is this information helpful?

What are the measurements of your new table and chair?

Furniture and clothes are designed for the average size person. Can you find out the average size of children in your class?

Look at your jumper or cardigan.
How long are the arms?
What is the chest measurement?
What material is it made from?

Design a cardigan that fits well and keeps you warm.
What would be the best material to use?

It's special!

These are the body bits and pieces of Jigsawman, a being from another planet. Match some of these pieces together and draw your own Jigsawman.

Jigsawman lives on a peaceful but bitterly cold planet. The surface is covered with sharp rocks and prickly plants. Jigsawman feeds on a small fruit that grows high up on a hill.

Can you help him?
Can you design a vehicle that takes him safely over the sharp rocks and the prickly plants to the fruit tree?

He needs a new suit to keep out the cold.
Design a suit that will keep him alive.

Imagine Jigsawman visiting Earth!
What language would you need to learn to talk to him?

What would he need in his survival pack to keep him alive on our planet?

Like you, Jigsawman is special!

31

Index

airliners	8	fading	11	rain gauge	16
arms	24, 30	feet	27	shadows	9
automatic watering		fingerprints	27	shadow stick	12
device	20	furniture	30	solar energy	6–7, 8
breathing	28	hands	27	solutions	23
		hobbies	29	sun	6–7
capillary action	20	ideas	3	sun clocks	13
clouds	15			sundials	13
complementary colours	10	legs	24	surface tension	19
condensed water	14	light meter	9	sweating	21
data pack	25	mass clock	12	time	12, 13
drops	18	pinhole viewer	9	water cycle	14
equipment	5	plants	13	water treatment	22
evaporation	14	protection against water	17	water vapour	14, 15
eye colour	26				

32